250 More Continuous-Line Quilting Designs

for Hand, Machine & Long-Arm Quilters

Laura Lee Fritz

C&T PUBLISHING

Copyright © 2002 by C&T Publishing
Editor: Cyndy Lyle Rymer
Technical Editor: Gael Betts
Book Design: Staci Harpole, Cubic Design
Cover Design: Christina Jarumay
Graphic Illustrations: Kirstie McCormick
Design Direction: Diane Pedersen
Production Assistant: Kristy A. Konitzer
Photography: Sharon Risendorph
Cover Images: Quilted images by Laura Lee Fritz

Attention Teachers:
C&T Publishing, Inc. encourages you to use this book as a text for teaching. Contact us at 800-284-1114 or www.ctpub.com for more information about the C&T Teachers Program.

Library of Congress Cataloging-in-Publication Data
Published by C&T Publishing, Inc.
P.O. Box 1456
Lafayette, California 94549

Fritz, Laura Lee.
  250 more continuous-line quilting designs for hand, machine & longarm
quilters / Laura Lee Fritz.
    p. cm.
  ISBN 1-57120-146-7 (paper trade)
  1. Quilting. 2. Quilts--Design. I. Title: Two hundred fifty more
continuous-line quilting designs for hand, machine & longarm quilters.
  II. Title.
  TT835 .F757 2002
  746.46'041--dc21
                                    2002007775

Printed in the United States
10 9 8 7 6 5 4 3 2 1

Contents

What You Can Do with These Designs

You can add beauty and special meaning to your quilting projects by using the graceful continuous-line images shown in the following pages. Whether you are quilting by hand, home sewing machine, or with a long-arm machine, this collection of designs will be a generous resource library.

You can combine them with each other and with interesting background-filling textures, as shown in the quilted samples throughout the book.

Please enlarge or reduce any of the designs to use on your quilts, and feel free to arrange and combine these ideas with more of your own.

The Quilt Top as a Stage: Planning the Design

If you think of your quilt in terms of a stage, and the quilting designs as the actors on that stage, designing your overall quilting plan will be easy.

One design will act as the lead character on center stage, with a supporting cast of one or more secondary design ideas. Provide some backdrops, such as a background grid and some architecture, and your story will unfold.

Here are two examples.

Quilt an ocean liner (the lead character), add surf and maybe some clouds (the backdrop), and add the seagull as your supporting character.

Waiting for Santa

Ocean Voyager

Quilt a pair of yuletide stockings (the main character), hang them from the fireplace mantel (a touch of architecture to provide a sense of place), and add a few candles and presents for supporting characters. The apparatus in the fireplace for holding logs and kettles is only suggestive, and works as a backdrop.

Another traditional favorite, the Log Cabin pattern, is perfectly quilted using only the Blooming Fan (page 60) or Interlocking Zinnia texture (page 59).

Random Baptist

Interlocking Zinnia

Patriotic quilts of red, white, and blue stars are gaining popularity now, and the Fireworks texture would set those stars in motion, as would the Celestial Overall texture (page 61).

Some contemporary quilts don't require much added imagery to be effective. You may rely on a single texture in one color area, and a second texture for the other. For example, a weaver fever is a bargello of two color planes zigzagging across the quilt. I would choose a vertical/horizontal straight-line texture opposite a curvy-loopy texture to accentuate the change in direction. For a stack-'n-whack quilt, quilt the background with one texture, and the pinwheel fabrics with another.

Transparent designs combine interesting shapes, but they are not made up of recognizable imagery. An overall meandering design is one example. Because of their simplicity, transparent designs don't jump out at you as you study a quilt.

Fireworks

You can also combine recognizable images with transparent designs; floating an occasional oak leaf on a still-waters texture is a subtle example of this blending of design ideas.

Sizing Your Designs

The primary quilt design for a block should fill about two-thirds of the block. If the background is closely quilted, a recessed dimension will make the primary design stand out more clearly. A loosely quilted background with a highly detailed primary image will have the opposite effect; the background will puff up around the detailed image.

Negative Space

Unquilted areas of a quilt are referred to as negative space. Between your leaves and textures, for example, the blank shapes can be large or small, clumsy shapes or graceful. Be observant of them. A poorly balanced design will have a negative space that is confused with the image; a negative space can be so large that the quilt seems to be underquilted, or so small that the quilting lines are hard to interpret.

Hints for Repeated Images

When you repeat designs to create a row or border, connect the designs with part of your supporting or backdrop design.

If you are planning a leafy border, avoid using a "row" of leaves. Create a more natural look by tilting each leaf in a different direction. Varying the size— or shape—of the leaves will help them fit within the space of the border, and will make the design less static.

A row of leaves in varying directions looks more natural.

Transitional Quilting Lines

When you are planning the background design for the borders, consider "crossing the lines" into the quilt block area. This creates a smooth transition between the two areas, and you can work all your side borders as you progress down the quilt.

Keep transition and escape routes in mind; they need to be consistent with the shape or feel of the background quilting in order to remain invisible.

Transferring the Designs

If you aren't ready to make the leap into free-motion quilting, there are simple steps to follow to transfer the designs onto your quilt top.

1. Trace the designs onto paper with a black permanent pen so you can use a copy machine to resize any image for your block or border. Trace the tracing again onto stencil plastic and cut it out with a "hot knife."

You may also trace the design onto bridal illusion (tulle), which is available at most of the larger chain fabric stores.

Both of these methods are a means to draw directly onto your quilt top with chalk, washout pencil, clean-erase pencil or a water/air soluble pen.

2. You can also trace your designs onto water-soluble stabilizer with a water-soluble pen and quilt through it as the topmost layer of your quilt. Try the Solvy stabilizers made by Sulky®, or Dissolve™ from Superior Threads, as they really do wash out of the cloth.

Dissolve can be used to accurately draw and quilt images onto quilts, and to lubricate tender threads for use on difficult fabrics. Draw on Dissolve's smooth side with a Sharpie pen—black only! Because of the nature of the medium, the pen line will not bleed through onto the source material. The complete transparency of Dissolve makes it easy to place the film over a quilt area, choosing to keep stitching lines from riding over seam junctions. If the project is a whole-cloth quilt larger than the 47" width, two pieces can be joined by ironing (use a press cloth) the bumpy sides to each other. In that case you will draw on the smooth side of one piece, and the bumpy side of the other, but you will hardly notice the difference if you are using the wider fine-point pen; only the ultra-fine-point pen will stumble on the miniscule bumps.

The toughness of Dissolve makes it easy to pin securely to the quilt. Pin well enough that your stitching in all directions will not cause the film to travel with the sewing line. Sew directly over your drawn line, except where you want to intentionally revise the image to fit your block, or make a corrective revision where you may have veered away from your intended path. An example of that circumstance would be if you veered from a line coming up the leg of a bird image; you'd be able to intentionally veer off the other side of the leg to keep it from being too skinny or too wide.

To remove the Dissolve from an isolated quilting of an image, simply rip it away from the quilt. Some of it will remain in small details. You can pick at it with the large eye of an embroidery needle or your fingernails in areas where you don't want to add water. Otherwise, spritz it with a spray of water or dab a water drop with your fingertip to dissolve the remnants.

Sew directly on your pattern lines. Pull away the largest chunks of the plastic-like material, then mop up the remaining fragments with a wet piece of cloth or a damp scrap of cotton/poly blend batting. I prefer using the batting to mop up because it holds water, scrubs without roughing up your quilt top, and doesn't leave shreds of itself behind.

*A **warning:** If you leave larger pieces of the Solvy or Dissolve on the quilt after dampening, they will turn to slime and dry on the quilt; the quilt will need a thorough washing.*

To remove a sheet of Dissolve used to quilt a whole-cloth design, it is easier to toss the whole project into a wash basin or washing machine and launder it off. Simply spraying a large area with water is going to melt it into the fabric like a plastic coating rather than remove it, so remember, spritz and rip, or wash it away.

Another use for Dissolve is to lubricate your stitching line over difficult fabrics. Some threads are too tender to quilt onto high thread-count cottons, such as some batiks. Other fabrics that torture thread include: the white-on-whites (and white on colors) that have a generous application of the white print (which is really a layer of paint); fusible appliqués; glitters applied to fabric with a glue surface; photo transfers (the stiff ones); and decorator prints that have heavy stain-proof coatings. These surfaces, and the cheap finishes from dollar-a-yard fabrics, act as a knife edge against the threads. By pinning on a layer of Dissolve over these trouble spots, those tender threads can be used without breaking.

3. Another option is to draw directly onto your quilt top with a washable marker. You will need a light source for this method.

> *Tip: A recycled sliding-window pane (still framed) or glass door panel from a shower enclosure will serve you well as a light table.*
>
> *Lay this glass panel over a quilt frame or sawhorse set, place a light source such as a four foot fluorescent shop light below the "table." Now spread your quilt top on top of the glass and turn the light on.*
>
> *Slide your drawings under the quilt, and position as desired.*
>
> *It becomes evident that clean white paper and bold black drawing lines will project best through the cloth.*

In time this tracing will train your eye and hand, and you can draw your own patterns to increase your collection.

Tools to Make Your (Quilting) Life Easier

Some materials and tools have been designed to make home-machine quilting easier. Here are a few you may find helpful.

I use a wide variety of threads and needles, and feel that experimentation is the best way to decide your favorites. I recommend Harriet Hargrave's *Heirloom Machine Quilting* as a source of information for any supplies.

The tools for small machine quilting are many. The simplest "rule" to remember is that any of the modern threads can be used by choosing a needle to be larger than the thread so the thread won't get roughed up or overheated during its journey in and out of the fabric.

- In the $15-$20 range you can find stenographers' rubber finger tips, or rubber-spotted cotton gloves; both provide a non-grip, non-slip contact with your quilt sandwich as you slide the quilt over the machine throat.

- I recommend cotton batting because it sticks well to cotton fabric, which allows for less basting. But be sure to follow the manufacturer's directions for the amount of basting you do.

- Sullivan and Sulky make basting adhesive sprays to hold your quilt layers together; use a light spray or you may get a sticky needle.

- Both the Flynn Multi Frame and HandiQuilter solve the problems of holding the quilt layers so you don't get them pleated, and holding the layers so that you can smoothly move them under your sewing machine needle.

  Both systems have three roller frames to hold your quilt. You slide the quilt under your darning foot before closing up the end of the frames.

  To work larger patterns than will fit within the reach of your sewing machine throat, you scroll your quilt along the rollers back and forth as you progress.

Using Border Designs

Once you choose a border design, you have three decisions to make: what direction to face the design; how to space or fit the border pattern to the length of the fabric border; and what to do in the corners.

1. Are all borders to be viewed in the same direction? A wall quilt would be so viewed, in which case the borders all have the top of the design facing the same way (you would have to customize the borders considerably to make them run vertically, but it gets done all the time). Or is it a throw quilt and the borders could all face outward or inward? A bed quilt may look great with a border across the pillows, with the top to the head of the bed; the lower border would also have its top to the head, and side borders top to the middle, so when viewed from the sides they are right side up.

2. Fit the border images within the span of the border. If the length of fabric causes you to end mid-image, then choose a "tight" spot between two images to extend a simple line an extra 1/4"–3/4" to spread the border. Repeat the spread each time you come to the same repeat in the border. This means doing a little math: If you need 4" more on a border design that is repeated nine times, then add 1/2" between each repeat eight times. In the same manner, you can shrink space between images, and repeat the shrinkage each time you come to a repeat of the place you compacted the design. The spread or compaction may be different for the side borders than for the top/bottom borders, as the border length will be different.

An alternative to spreading or shrinking is to divide the border design in half, with half of it facing the other in a mirror image. If you choose this route, add an extra design between them in the middle of the border span. An example of this is the Flower Buds border on page 53 that is already drawn that way.

Spacing borders as an overall repeat of the row means you also need to see how much space remains, if any, after you determine the number of repeats. If you can fit nine repeats of a border design with 4" left over, you would spread each row apart by a half inch. Here is the formula for figuring the amount to spread the designs: Take the number of inches you need to fill (what is "left over" after all the full repeats), and divide it by how many "spaces" between the repeats. So 6" divided by nine "spaces" (ten rows of design) would mean I need to space the rows apart by 2/3", or, for ease of measuring, just less than 3/8".

3. Corner designs may be added to provide a transition between the horizontal and vertical borders. Ideally one of the images in the border will fit the corner block. You may draw a simple curved connecting line between each of the two borders, sometimes getting a bit creative when choosing where to connect the lines. You may choose a feature image or a background image, or possibly draw a new version of some idea in the border. Another possibility is to launch a new idea for a corner, such as a sunburst that joins the borders of birds at work in the surf.

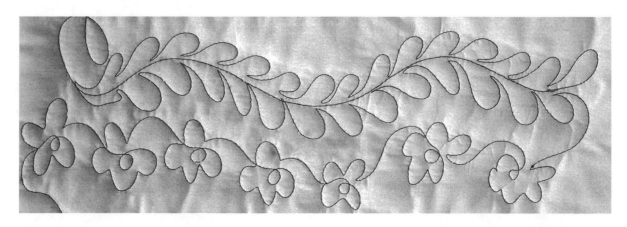

Customizing Your Projects

To achieve a refined look to your quilting, follow these designs with a stylus laser light (if you are working on a long-arm machine), or by stitching over a tracing you've drawn with a black Sharpie pen on Dissolve (or Solvy). Add any improvements to the design that might make you like it better.

> *Tip: Some lines are drawn "apart" to show you the stitching path, but you may get a lovelier pattern if you sew the lines closer together. When I draw the haunches of a horse, I like the big leg muscle to be outlined, but if I quilt a distinct space between the line going up around the muscle and the same outline returning to the horse's belly, it doesn't look as realistic as if I sew the entry and exit lines close enough to read as one outline.*

For a whimsical or a folk-art look, draw or quilt freehand, following the design that you have right in front of you. Looking at my first book in this series, you can tell where the editors sometimes chose my looser freehand quilting renditions rather than my drawings.

Create your own whole-block motifs by enlarging an image (or set of images) to fill the block to within an inch of the seams. All the areas within the block that are not filled with the image need to be completed. Could a secondary image be added to fill the blanks?

Or an opposing-direction texture be used as fill? What about adding an extension or flourish to the design to complete the block? The goal is to not leave any area unquilted that would loft above the feature design, competing for center stage. Connect all the design areas you add to the main image(s).

To join various designs to make your own borders, find the idea that connects the images: Flowers may connect insects together, leaves connect flowers, a landscape connects horses, or prairie grasses connect pheasants. Be sure to make your drawings of the connecting imagery large enough to fill the negative spaces.

A design can be "entered" from many choices of location: Any foot of a horse provides two entry points; its tail provides another entry point. To start a horse image near the face or along its back would be distracting. Try some options and choose the least noticeable one.

For machine quilting, how do you get a perfect stitch length? Just pay attention as you work, and practice before doing an intricate design.

Sometimes you will need to slow your needle speed for the shorter-line designs (the insect) and speed it up again for the long smooth shapes (the calla lily next to the insect). Practice will show you where you need to pay more attention, and where you need to change your speed to control stitch and shape quality.

Funky Chickens

Start Quilting

You just need to practice machine quilting in order to find your rhythm, and learn to sew at a constant speed.

> **Warm-up Tip:** *Begin by tracing the designs with your fingertips or a pencil to practice the paths, and you will learn to stitch many of them free-hand. This tracing makes the pattern a physical memory and helps you quilt more smoothly.*
>
> **How to Begin Sewing a Continuous-Line Quilting Design:** *Note any pattern sections where you change sewing direction, sew over an area twice, or sew over an existing line of stitching. You may find it helpful to draw arrows using a highlighter marker on the pattern to guide you.*
>
> *For most of the patterns the starting and stopping points are indicated. You can start at either end of the pattern and sew left to right or right to left.*
>
> *Match points (registration marks) are provided for continuous borders and textures. You may want to sketch the continuation of the pattern at the match point so it is clear to your mind's eye which direction you will sew to continue the pattern.*

When you start or end a line of quilting, or when your top thread or bobbin is depleted, knot the end(s) of your stitching line and thread a needle with the thread tails. Use a long-eye sharp embroidery needle for the tail so both threads will fit through at once. Try wrapping the pair of threads around the eye tightly, pinch the thread to hold the tiny loops as you withdraw the needle, then slip the eye over these tight little loops. Sew these ends by sliding the needle back along your quilting line, pull the needle out, bury the knot into the batting, and cut the tail.

A Word About Art

Throughout history quilts have represented people's lives, often expressing a love of story as well as love of color. Many of us don't sit down to conjure up "pretty pictures," so we say, "I'm not an artist."

Being an artist is all in the practice of art. Those of us who make pretty lines attract people who value pretty lines. If we create bold, abstract lines we attract those who value that form. Folk art is a more spontaneous art form; we just need to make the story unfold. There are vast numbers of people who are attracted to folk art for its direct simplicity.

It is sufficient to practice your craft in an expressive way, and follow the path of just "doing it." You will begin to see the world with a greater attention to what it truly looks and feels like, and those observations will appear in your work. Now you are an artist.

> **Please Note:** *All designs featured in the black and white photographs can also be traced and used in your quilts.*

Spring

Baby Ducks in a Row

Mother Duck

Bird Bath

Duckling

Birds in Nest 2

Swan

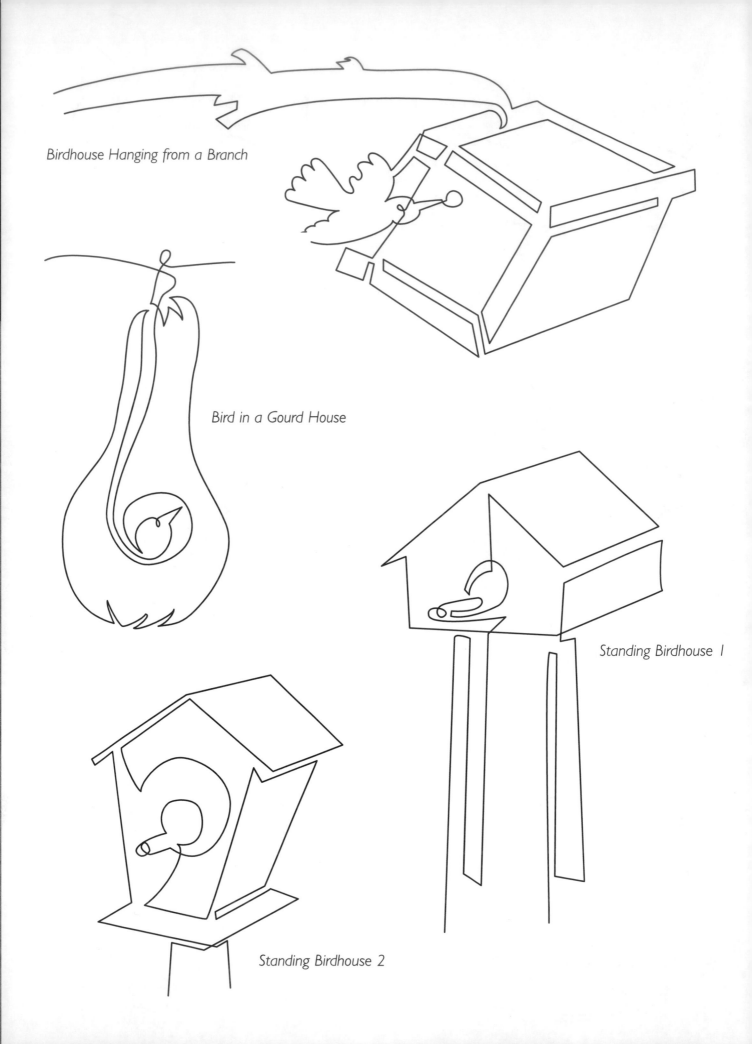

Birdhouse Hanging from a Branch

Bird in a Gourd House

Standing Birdhouse 1

Standing Birdhouse 2

Bunny with Basket

Butterfly 1

Bunny

Butterfly 2

Daffodils and Grape Hyacinth

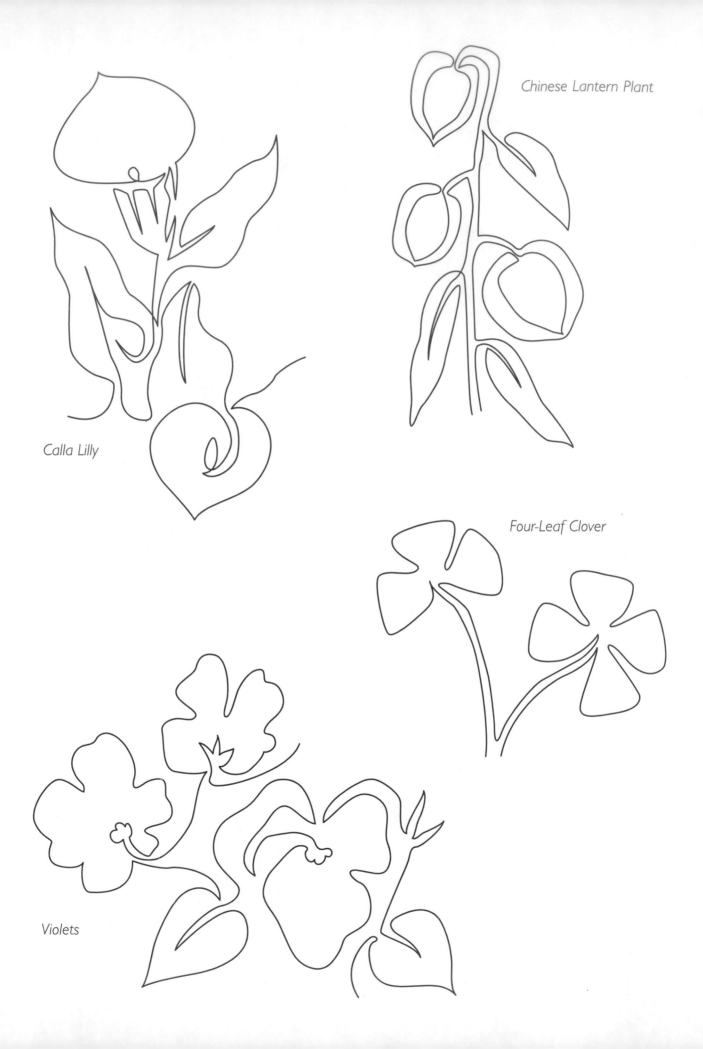

Chinese Lantern Plant

Calla Lilly

Four-Leaf Clover

Violets

Spring Basket

*Crocus and
Tulips*

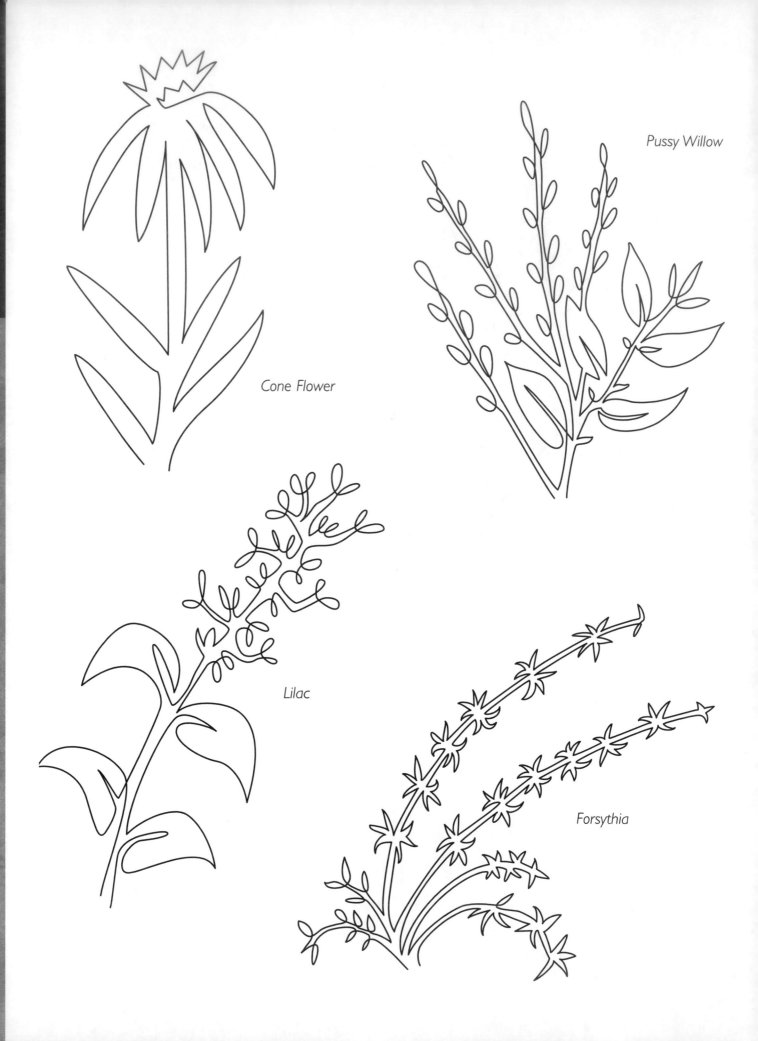

Cone Flower

Pussy Willow

Lilac

Forsythia

Shooting Star

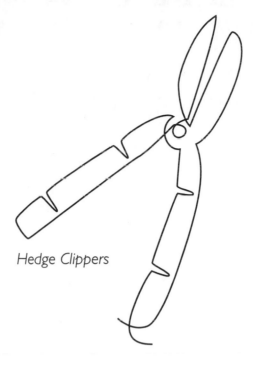

Hedge Clippers

Umbrella

Ball in Glove

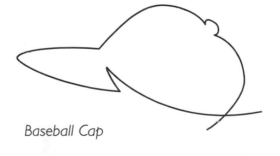

Baseball Cap

Summer

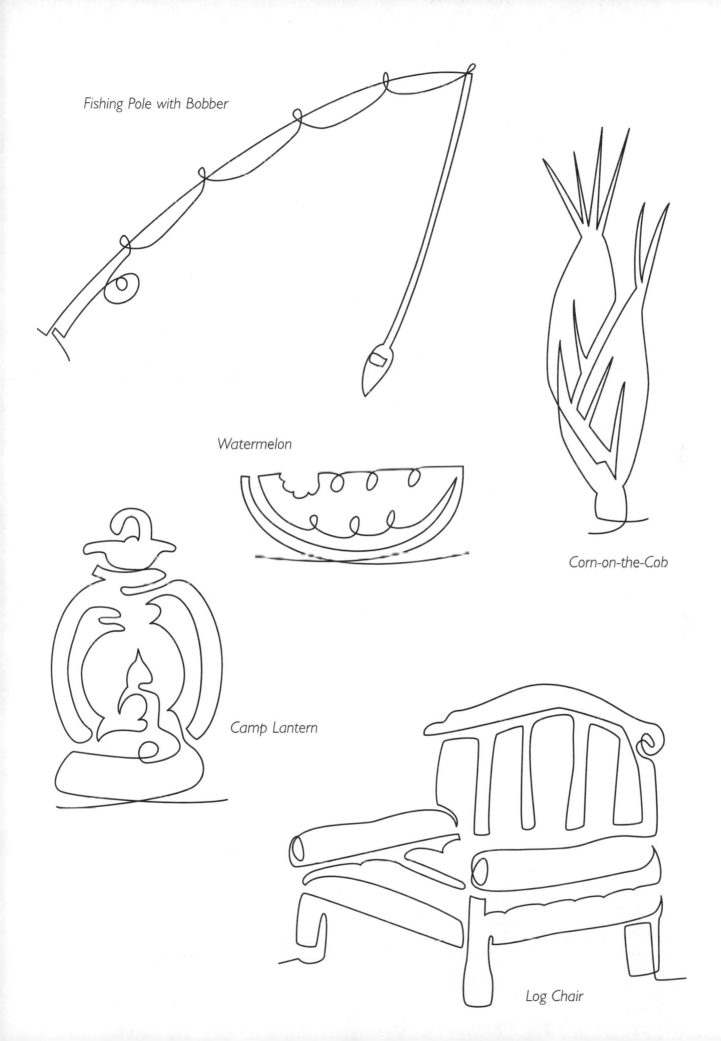

Fishing Pole with Bobber

Watermelon

Corn-on-the-Cob

Camp Lantern

Log Chair

Surfer

Woody with Surfboards

Bottle 2

Palm Trees

Lemonade

Bottle 1

Beach Chair

Lounge Chair

Seaplane

Bush Plane

Sailboat

24

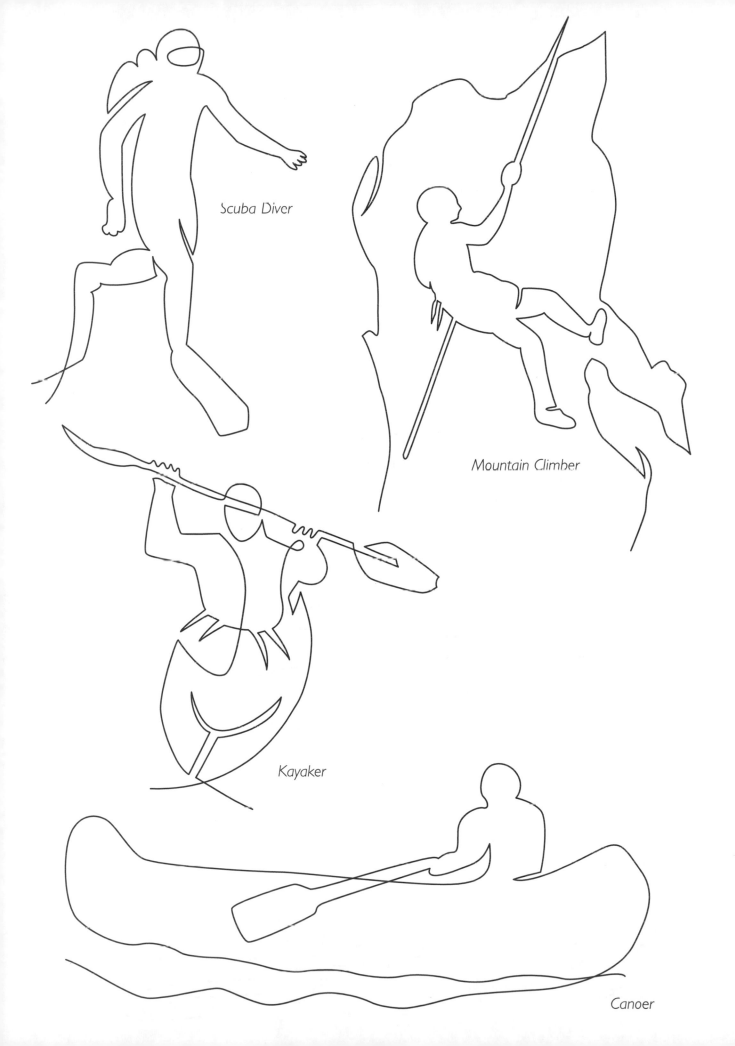

Scuba Diver

Mountain Climber

Kayaker

Canoer

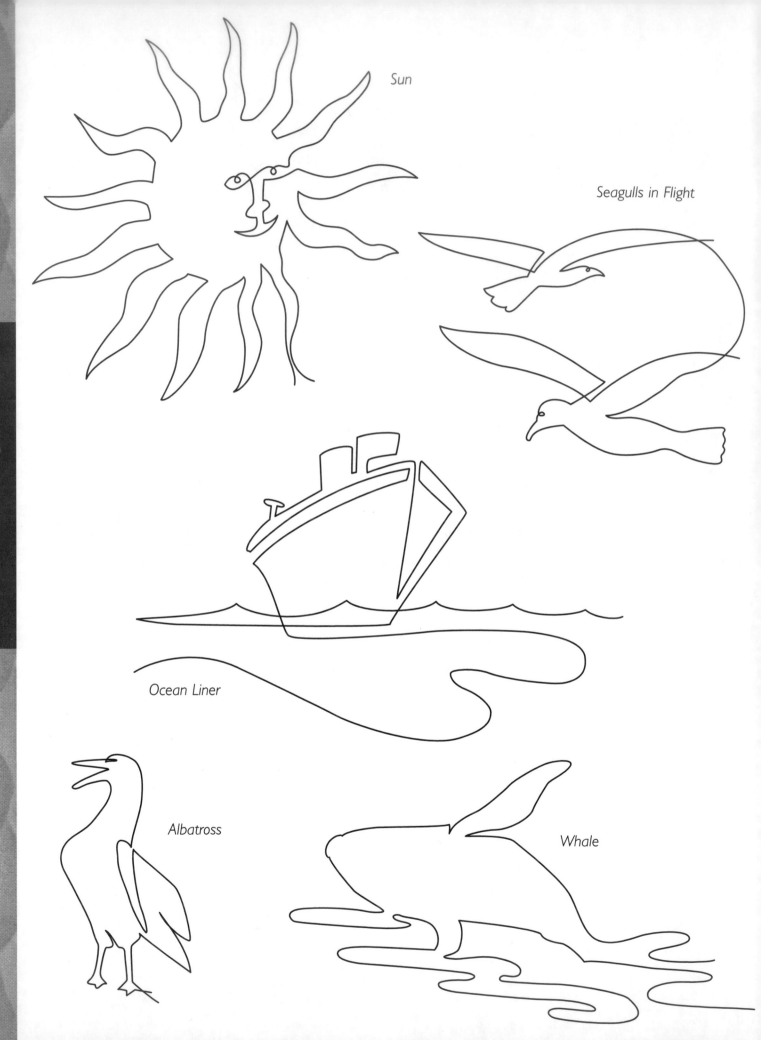

Sun

Seagulls in Flight

Ocean Liner

Albatross

Whale

Bird of Paradise

Gladiolas

Lily

American Eagle and Flag

Swallowtail

Kite

Roses

Cherry Tree

Honey Bee

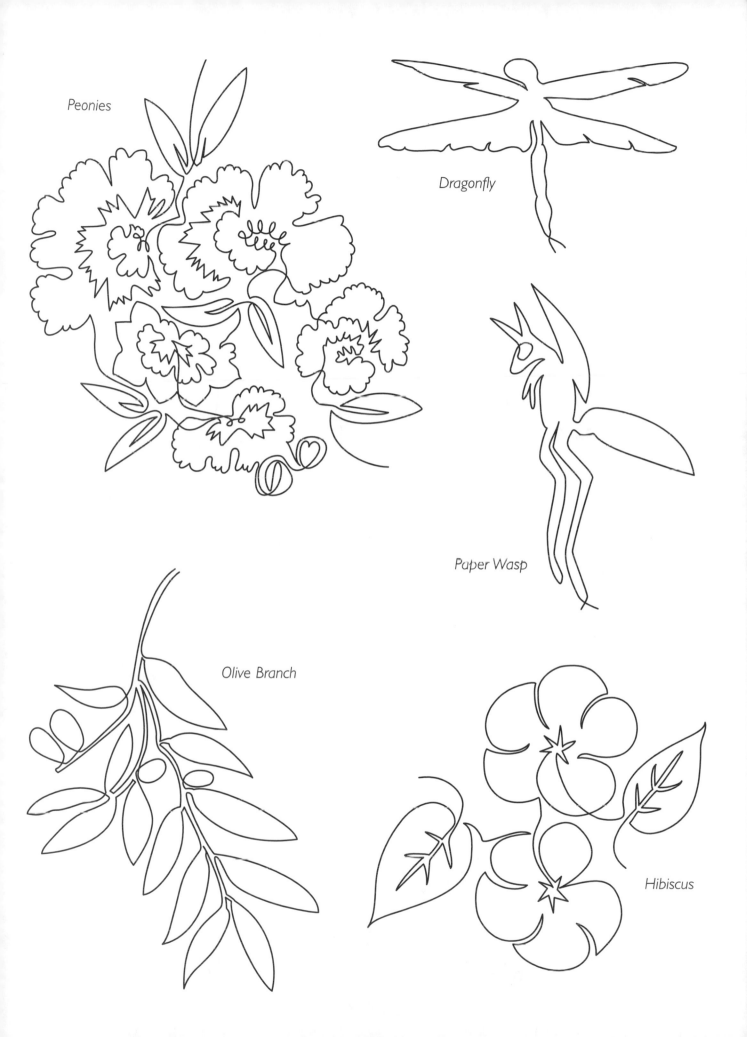

Peonies

Dragonfly

Paper Wasp

Olive Branch

Hibiscus

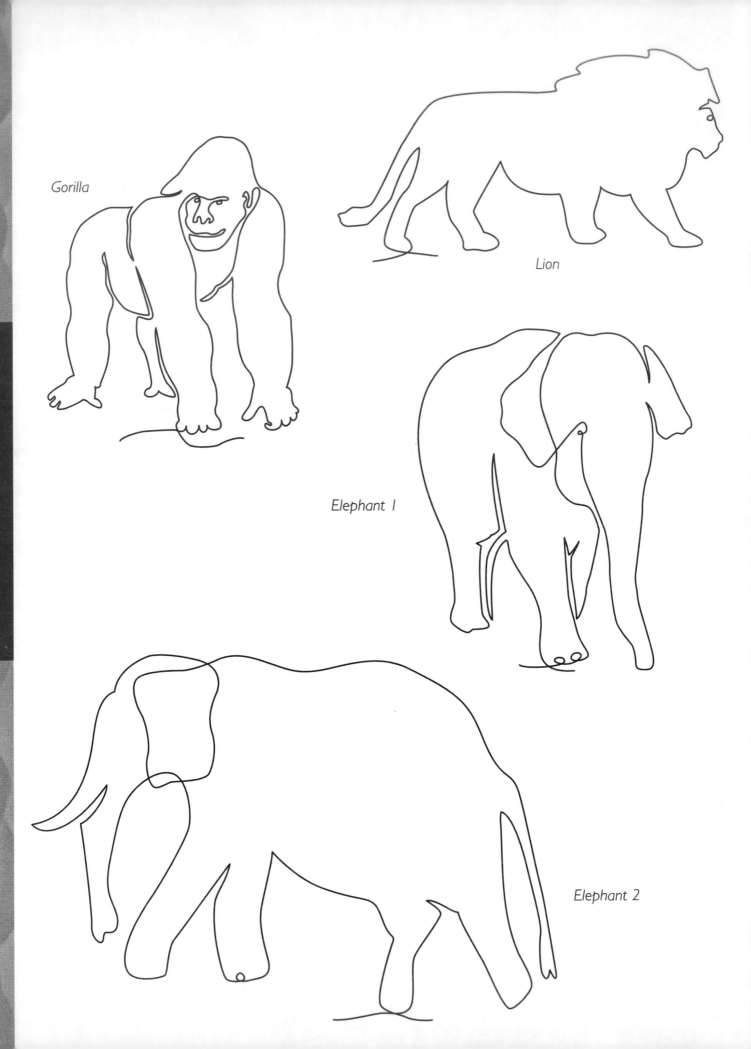

Gorilla

Lion

Elephant 1

Elephant 2

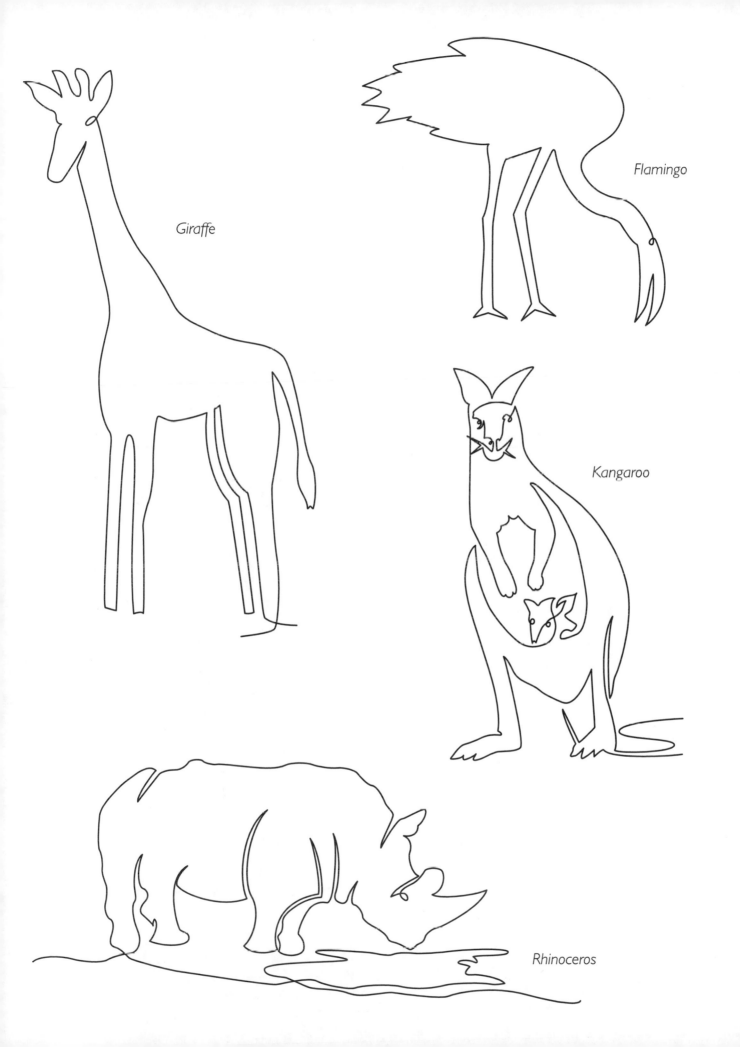

Giraffe

Flamingo

Kangaroo

Rhinoceros

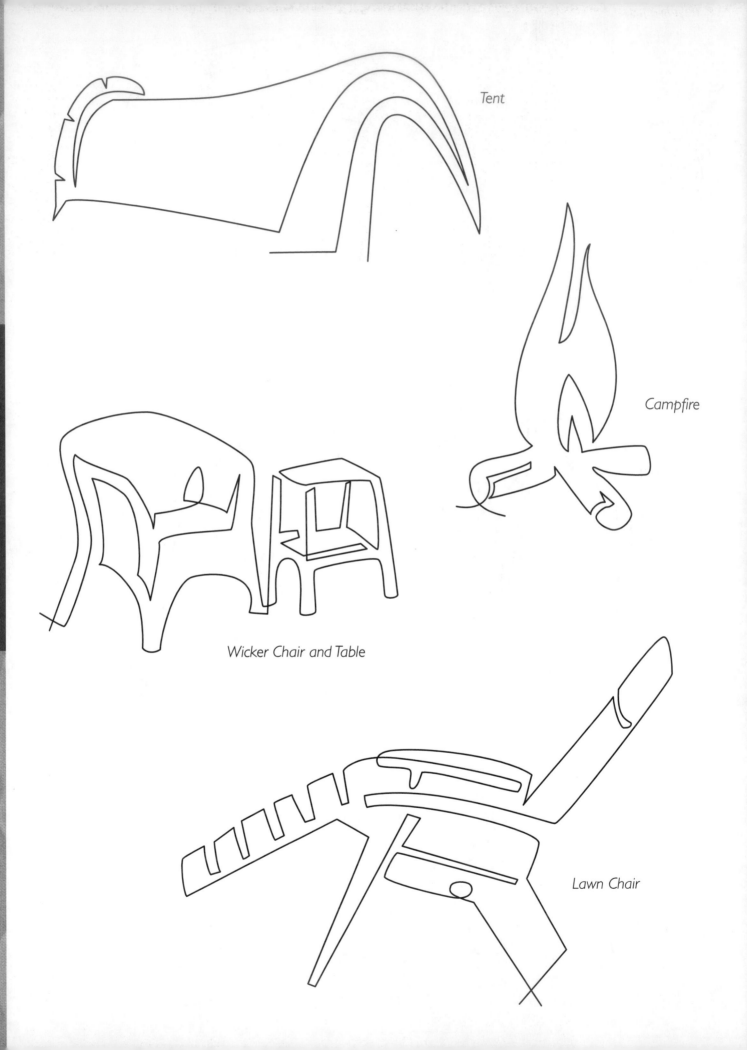

Tent

Campfire

Wicker Chair and Table

Lawn Chair

Fall

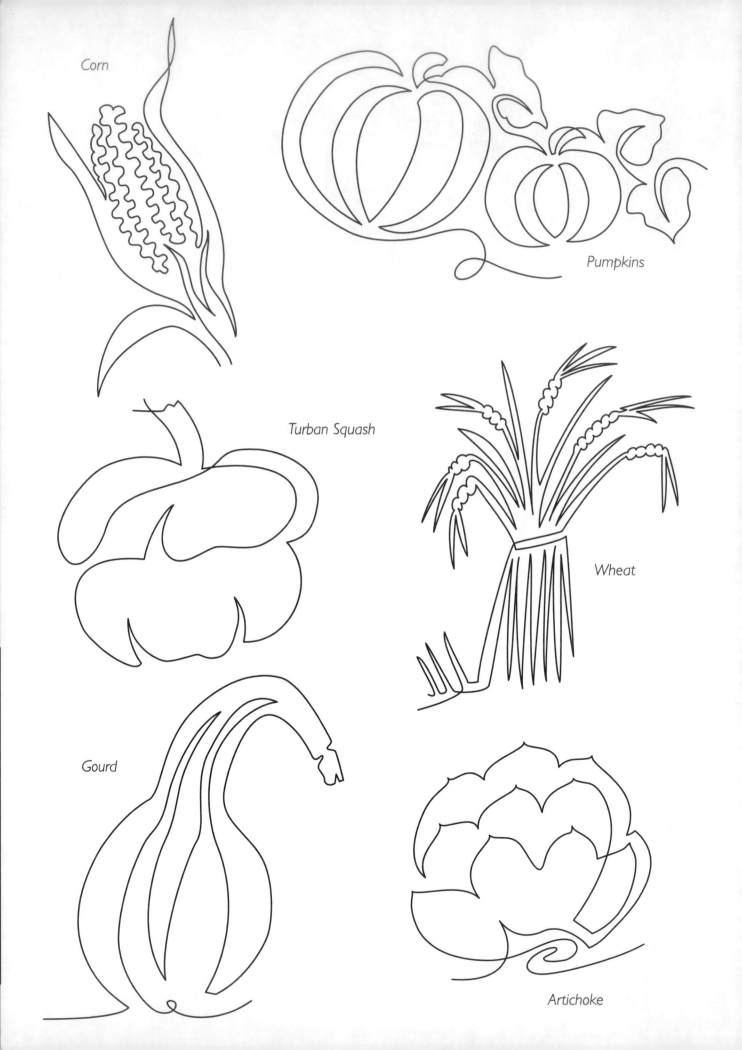

Corn

Pumpkins

Turban Squash

Wheat

Gourd

Artichoke

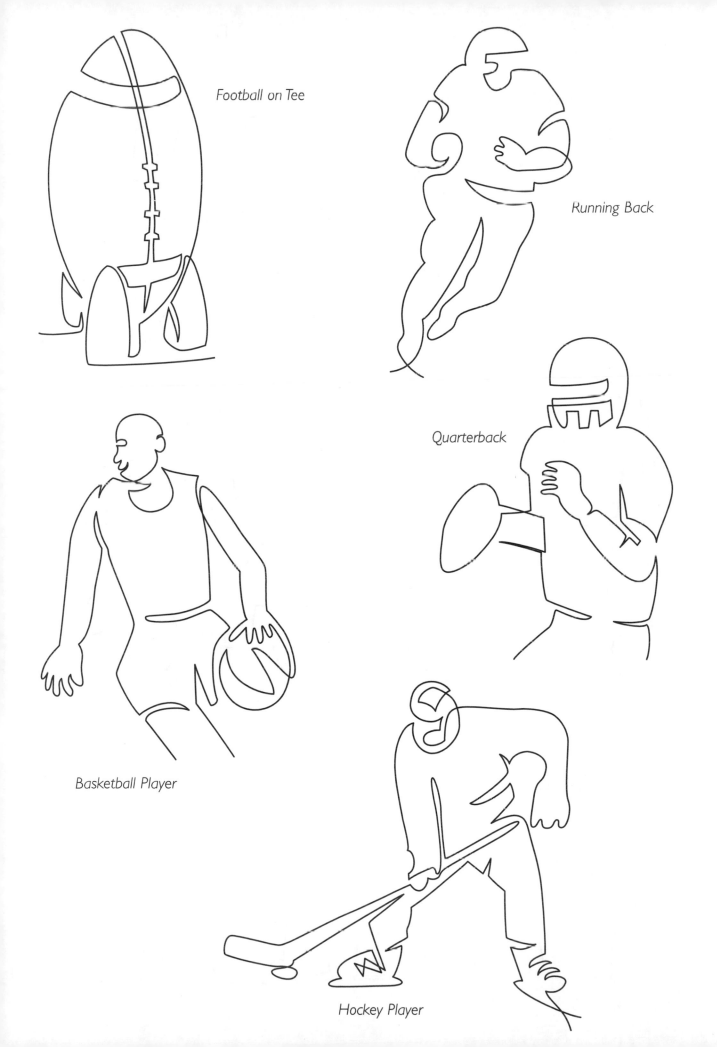

Football on Tee

Running Back

Quarterback

Basketball Player

Hockey Player

Tractor

Windmill

Payloader

Farmhouse and Haystacks

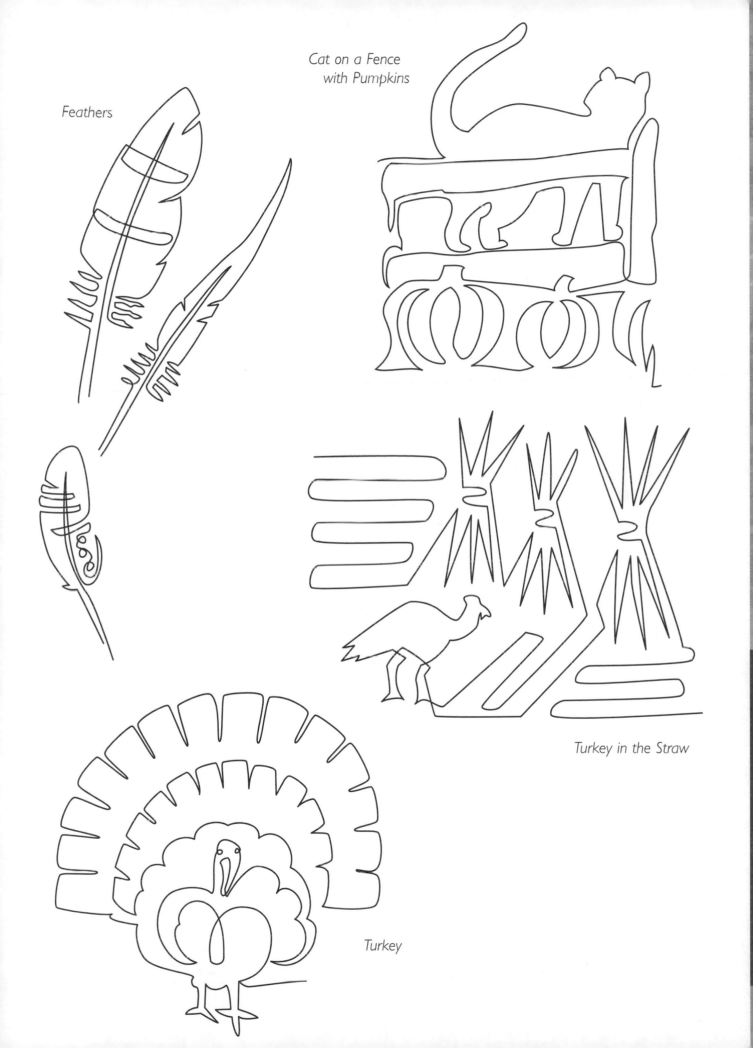

Feathers

Cat on a Fence
with Pumpkins

Turkey in the Straw

Turkey

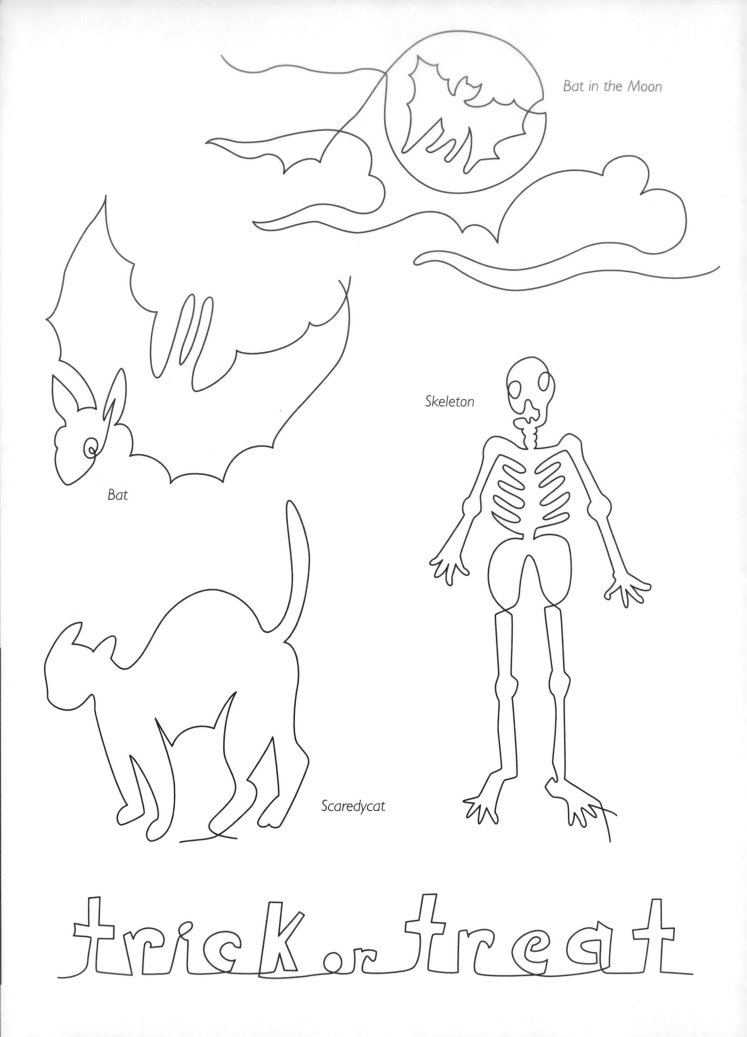

Bat in the Moon

Skeleton

Bat

Scaredycat

trick or treat

Wizard

Witch on a Broom

Owl

Ghost 1

Man-in-the Moon

Ghost 2

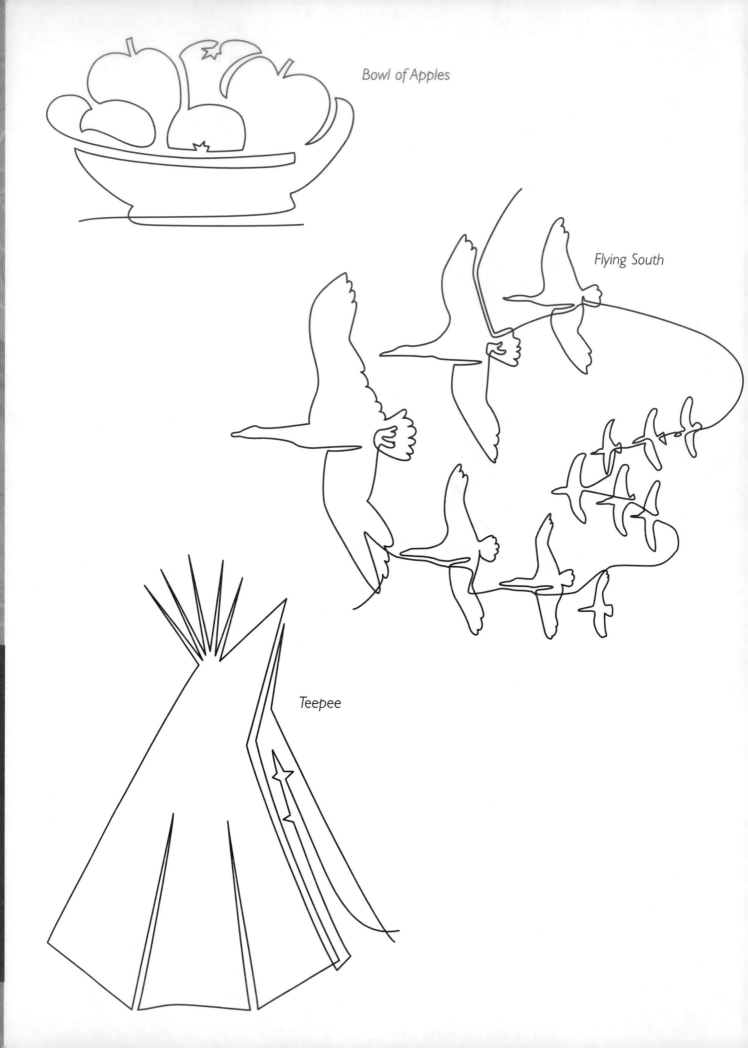

Bowl of Apples

Flying South

Teepee

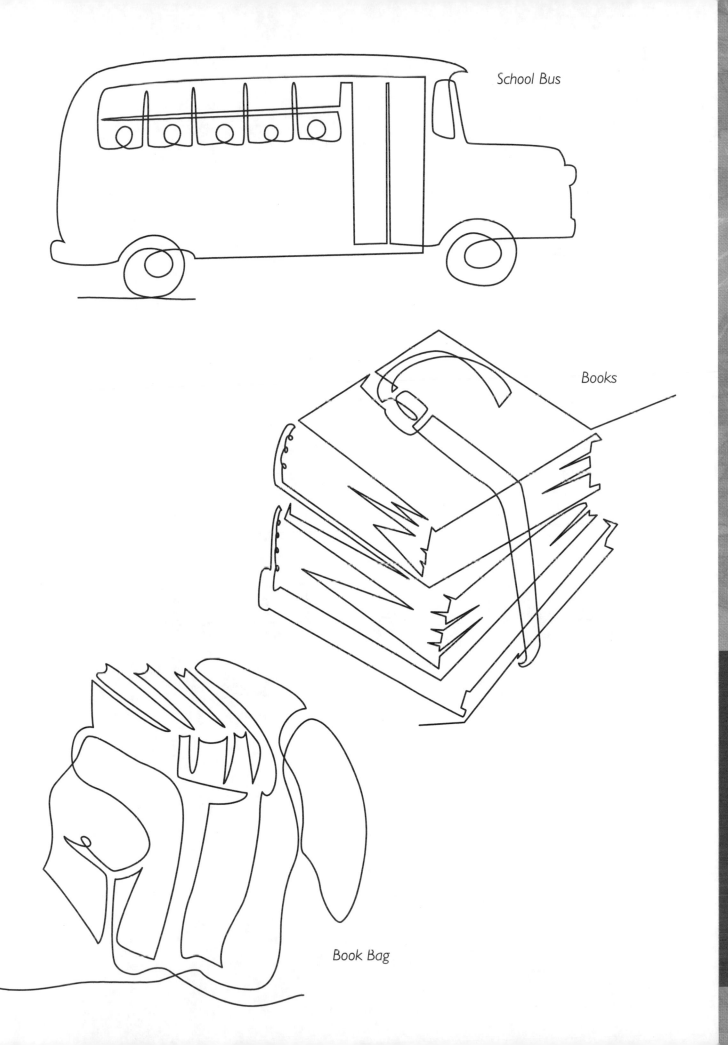

School Bus

Books

Book Bag

Winter

Menorah

Wise Men

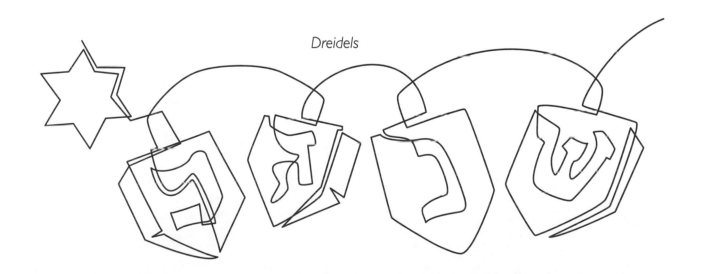

Dreidels

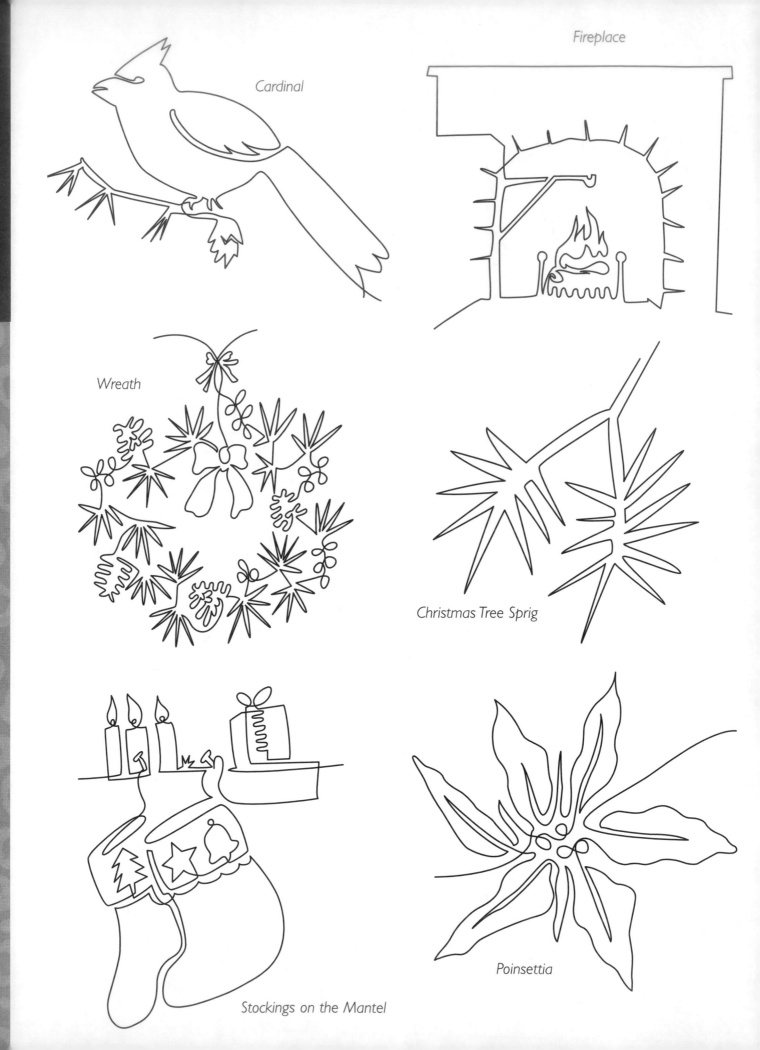

Winter

Cardinal

Fireplace

Wreath

Christmas Tree Sprig

Stockings on the Mantel

Poinsettia

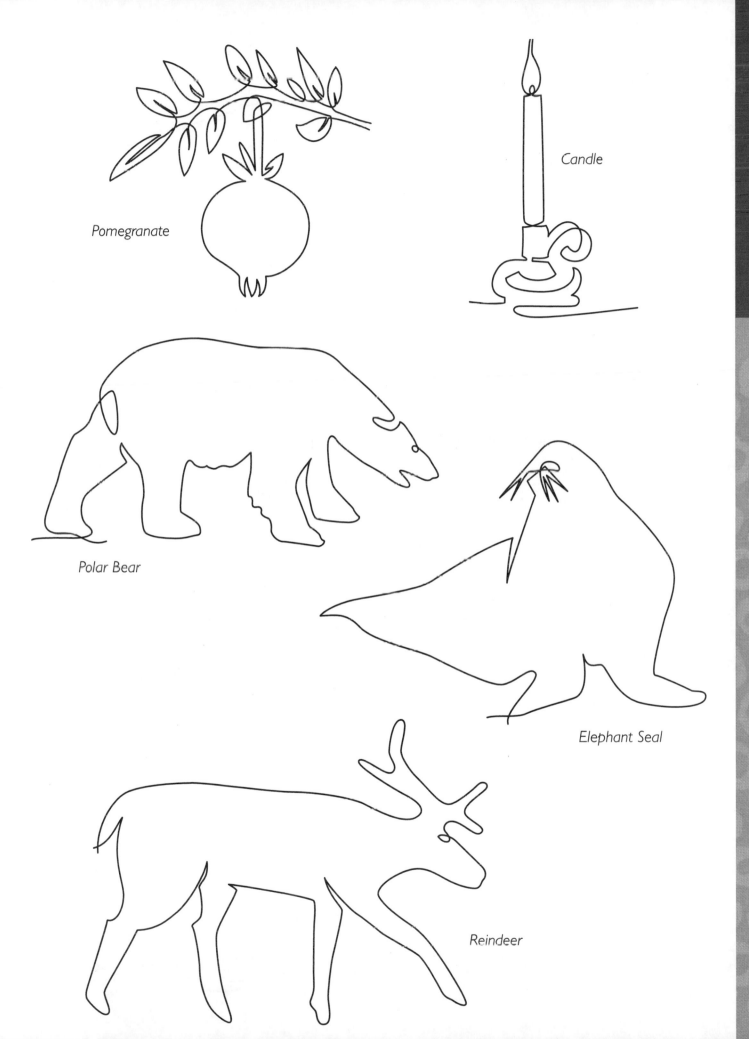

Pomegranate

Candle

Polar Bear

Elephant Seal

Reindeer

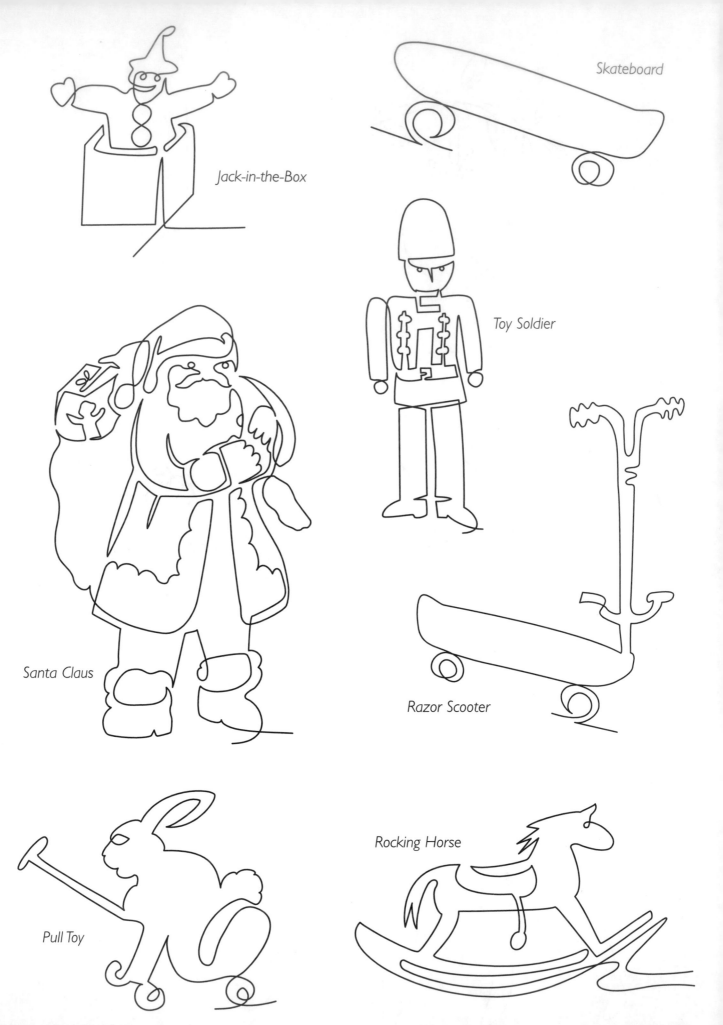

Jack-in-the-Box

Skateboard

Toy Soldier

Santa Claus

Razor Scooter

Pull Toy

Rocking Horse

Bicycle

Young Ballerina

Toy Plane 1

Ballerina

Angel

Mouse King

Toy Plane 2

Valentine

Row of Hearts

Cupid

Snowman

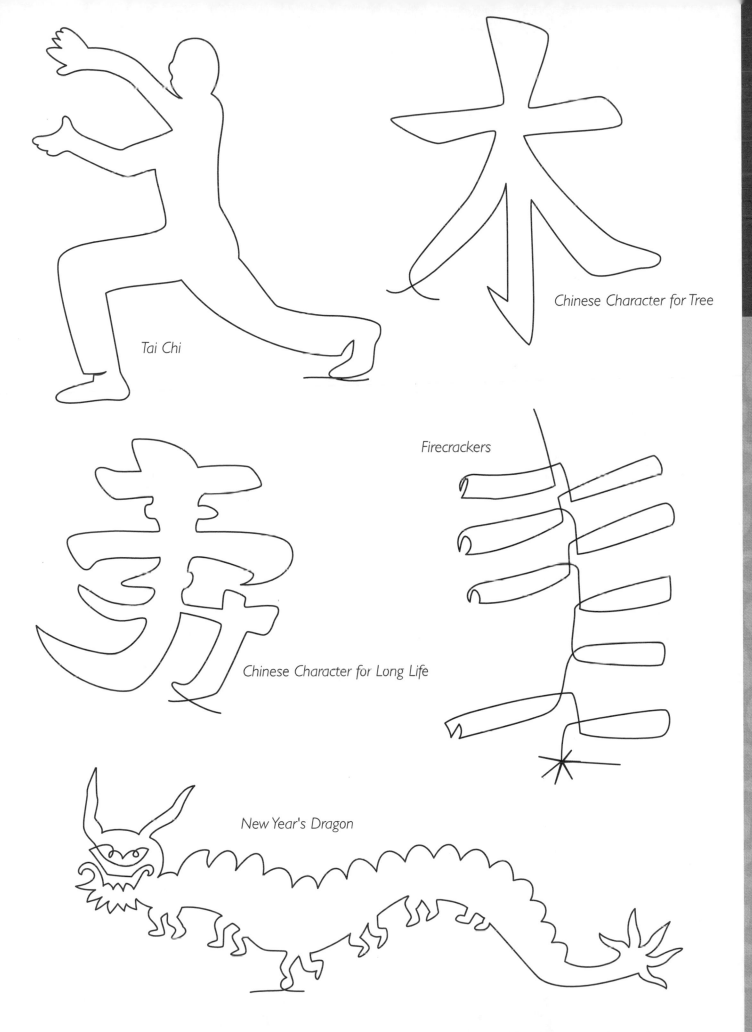

Tai Chi

Chinese Character for Tree

Firecrackers

Chinese Character for Long Life

New Year's Dragon

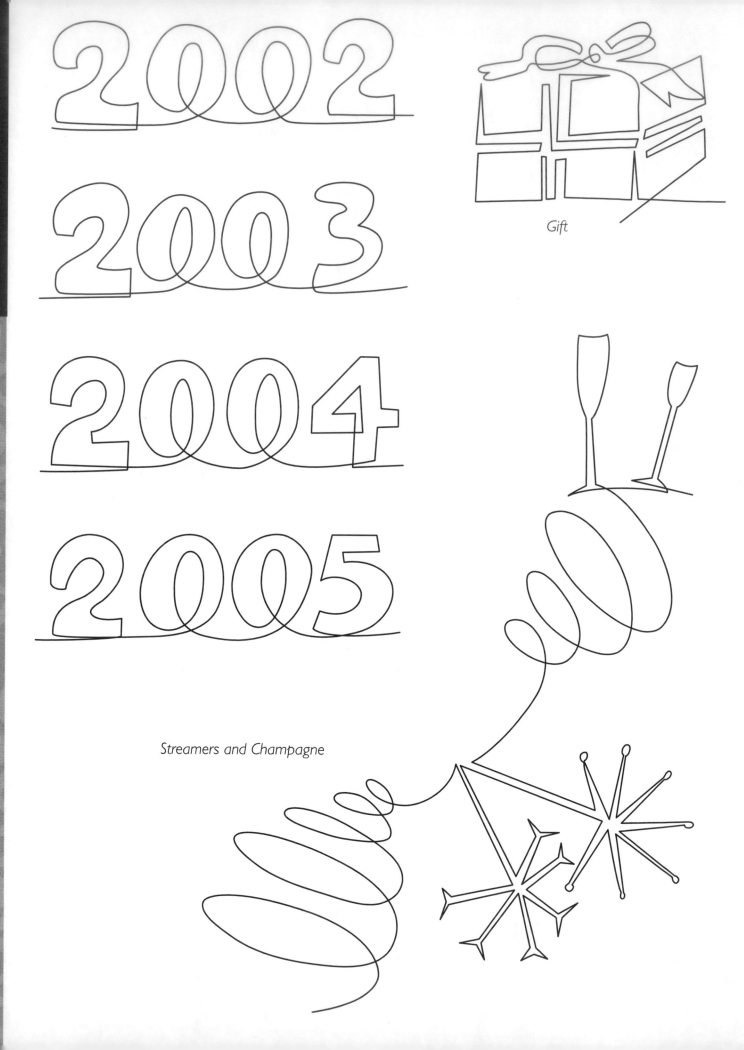

2002

2003

2004

2005

Gift

Streamers and Champagne

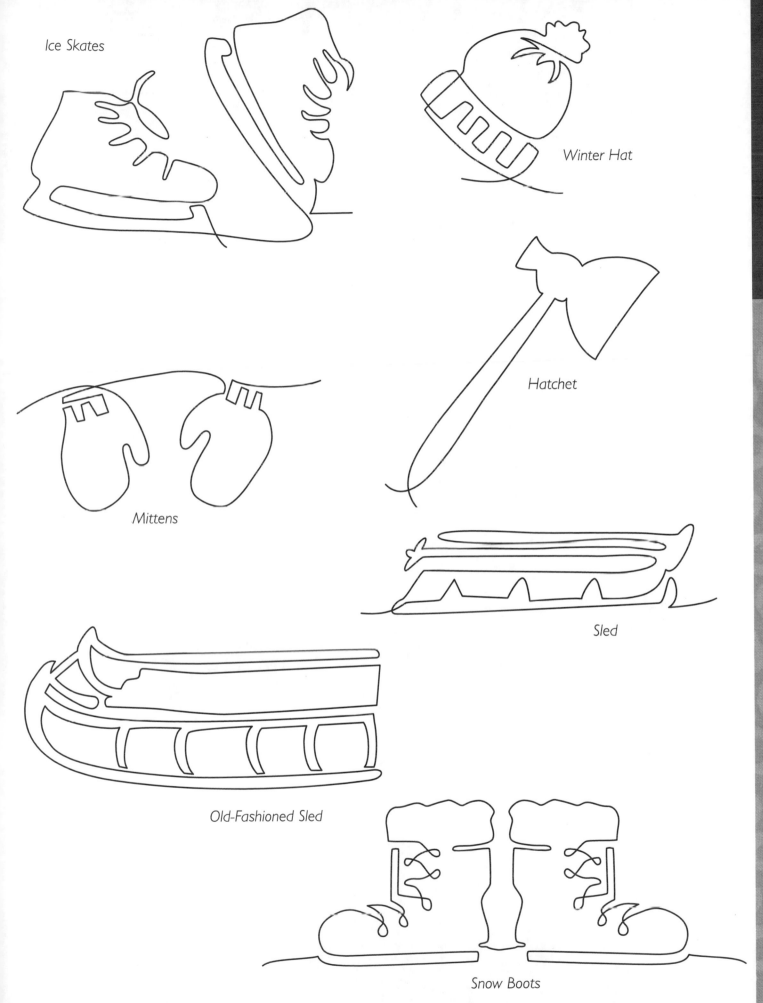

Ice Skates

Winter Hat

Hatchet

Mittens

Sled

Old-Fashioned Sled

Snow Boots

Borders

Cyclamen

Holly

Flower Buds

Daylilies

Tulips

Trees and Low Clouds

Bounding Deer

Leaves

Congratulations

Happy Birthday

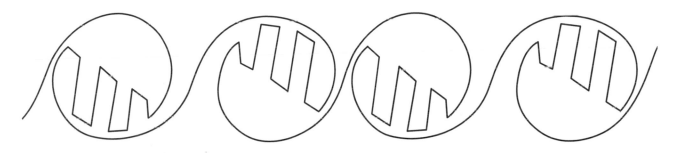

Art Deco Wheels

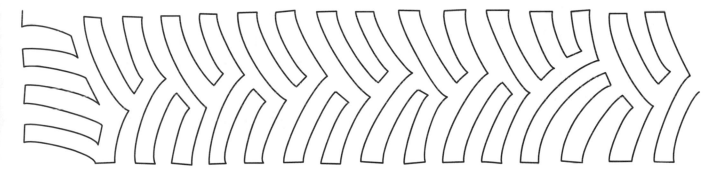

Braided Fan

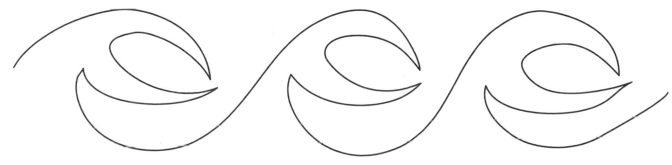

Casting Seeds

Celtic Fish in a Wave

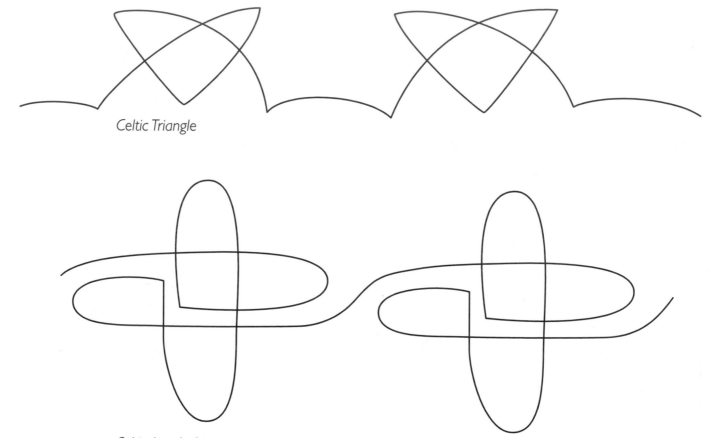

Celtic Triangle

Celtic Interlocking

Celtic Arrowheads

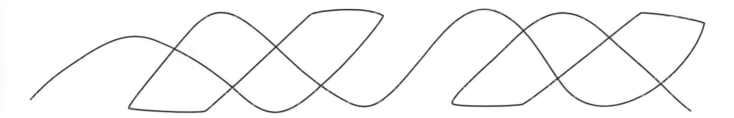

Celtic Border

Celtic Fish Knot

Cable Border

Textures

Half-Stars Overall

Interlocking Zinnia

Propeller

Blooming Fan

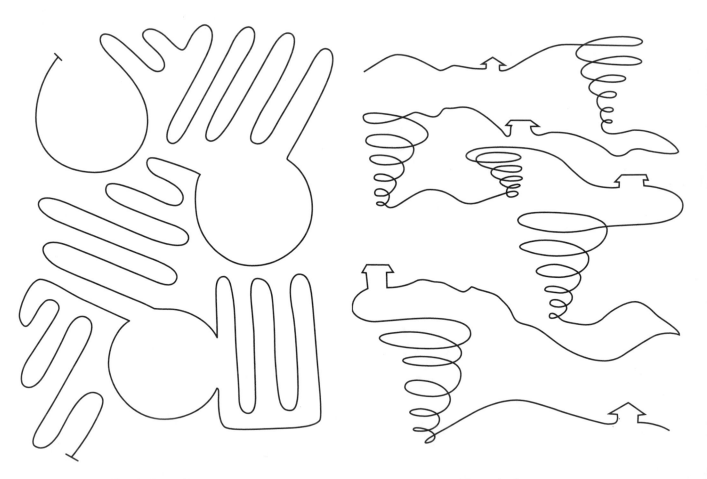

Fields from Above

Tornado Season

Fireworks

Celestial Overall

Alphabet

Hebrew Letters

About the Author

Laura Lee Fritz is widely known for her hand appliqué quilts and her fanciful wholecloth quiltings filled with narrative images from the stories surrounding her life. Laura raises alpacas and Navajo-Churro sheep in rural Middletown, California, but slips off of the farm to teach quilting classes everywhere—from her weekly class at a local college to her long-arm machine quilting classes at the annual International Quilt Festival in Houston.

Photo by Ron Paul.

Resources

American & Efird (A & E) Inc. (Threads)
400 East Central Ave.
Mount Holly, NC 28120
800-438-0545
www.amefird.com

Gammill Quilting Systems™
1452 West Gibson
West Plains, MS 65775
Gammill@townsqr.com

Hobbs Bonded Fibers
P.O. Box 2521
Waco, TX 76702

Kelsul Batting
3205 Foxgrove Lane
Chesapeake, VA 23321
888-268-8664

Superior Threads
P.O. Box 1672
St. George, UT 84771
800-499-1777
www.superiorthreads.com

The Warm Company
954 E. Union Street
Seattle, WA 98122
800-234-WARM
www.warmcompany.com

YLI Corporation
161 West Main St.
Rock Hill, SC 29730
800-296-8139
www.ylicorp.com

Other Fine Books from C&T Publishing

3-in-1 Color Tool, Joen Wolfrom

250 Continuous-Line Quilting Designs for Hand, Machine & Long-Arm Quilters, Laura Lee Fritz

America from the Heart: Quilters Remember September 11, 2001

A Bouquet of Quilts: Garden-Inspired Projects for the Home, edited by Jennifer Rounds & Cyndy Lyle Rymer

Butterflies & Blooms: Designs for Appliqué & Quilting, Carol Armstrong

Come Listen to My Quilts•Playful Projects •Mix & Match Designs, Kristina Becker

Cotton Candy Quilts: Using Feedsacks, Vintage and Reproduction Fabrics, Mary Mashuta

Enchanted Views: Quilts Inspired by Wrought-Iron Designs, Dilys A. Fronks

Hand Appliqué with Alex Anderson: Seven Projects for Hand Appliqué, Alex Anderson

Hand Quilting with Alex Anderson: Six Projects for Hand Quilters, Alex Anderson

Heirloom Machine Quilting, Third Edition, Harriet Hargrave
How to Machine Quilt: A Fun, No-Mark Approach, Kathy Sandbach

Mastering Machine Appliqué, 2nd Edition, Harriet Hargrave

On the Surface: Thread Embellishment & Fabric Manipulation, Wendy Hill

Quick Quilts for the Holidays: 11 Projects to Stamp, Stencil, and Sew, Trice Boerens

Quilting Back to Front: Fun & Easy No-Mark Techniques, Larraine Scouler

Quilting with Carol Armstrong: 30 Quilting Patterns, Appliqué Designs, 16 Projects, Carol Armstrong

A Thimbleberries Housewarming:22 Projects for Quilters, Lynette Jensen

Trapunto by Machine, Hari Walner

Wild Birds: Designs for Appliqué & Quilting, Carol Armstrong

Wildflowers: Designs for Appliqué & Quilting, Carol Armstrong

Women of Taste: A Collaboration Celebrating Quilts, Artists, and Chefs, Girls Incorporated

For more information write for a free catalog:
C&T Publishing, Inc.
P.O. Box 1456
Lafayette, CA 94549
(800) 284-1114
e-mail: ctinfo@ctpub.com
website: www.ctpub.com

For quilting supplies:
Cotton Patch Mail Order
3405 Hall Lane, Dept. CTB
Lafayette, CA 94549
(800) 835-4418
(925) 283-7883
e-mail: quiltusa@yahoo.com
website: www.quiltusa.com